First Facts®

National Landmarks

THE
VIETNAM VETERANS
MEMORIAL

A 4D BOOK

by Erin Edison

PEBBLE
a capstone imprint

Download the Capstone app!

- Ask an adult to download the Capstone 4D app.
- Scan the cover and stars inside the book for additional content.

When you scan a spread, you'll find fun extra stuff to go with this book! You can also find these things on the web at www.capstone4D.com using the password: vvmemorial.31329

First Facts are published by Pebble
1710 Roe Crest Drive, North Mankato, Minnesota 56003
www.mycapstone.com

Library of Congress Cataloging-in-Publication Data
Names: Edison, Erin, author.
Title: The Vietnam Veterans Memorial : a 4D book / by Erin Edison.
Description: North Mankato, Minnesota : Pebble, a Capstone imprint, 2019. |
    Series: First facts. National landmarks
Identifiers: LCCN 2018004149 (print) | LCCN 2018012030 (ebook) | ISBN
    9781543531404 (eBook PDF) | ISBN 9781543531329 (hardcover) | ISBN
    9781543531367 (pbk.)
Subjects: LCSH: Vietnam Veterans Memorial (Washington, D.C.)—Juvenile
    literature. | Vietnam War, 1961–1975—United States—Juvenile literature.
    | War memorials—Washington (D.C.)—Juvenile literature. | Washington
    (D.C.)—Buildings, structures, etc.—Juvenile literature.
Classification: LCC DS559.83.W18 (ebook) | LCC DS559.83.W18 E35 2019 (print)
    | DDC 959.704/36—dc23
LC record available at https://lccn.loc.gov/2018004149

Editorial Credits
Erika L. Shores, editor; Sarah Bennett, designer; Eric Gohl, media researcher;
Tori Abraham, production specialist

Photo Credits
AP Photo: Ira Schwarz, 15; Getty Images: Bettmann, 7, 11, 13, Diana Walker, 17, Larry Burrows, 9; iStockphoto: Coast-to-Coast, 21; Library of Congress: 12; Shutterstock: DavidNNP, 5 (bottom), Gang Liu, 20, GiuseppeCrimeni, cover, Marco Rubino, 19, PSboom, 5 (top), travelview, 18

Design Elements: Shutterstock

Printed and bound in the United States of America.
PA017

Table of Contents

Honoring Vietnam Veterans

The Vietnam **Veterans Memorial** is in Washington, D.C. People visit it to remember those who **served** in the Vietnam War.

The memorial has three parts. The Wall was built first. *The Three Servicemen* statue and the Vietnam Women's Memorial were added later.

veteran—a person who served in the armed forces

memorial—something that is built or done to help people remember a person or event

serve—to work as a member of the armed forces

United States of America

WASHINGTON
OREGON
MONTANA
NORTH DAKOTA
MINNESOTA
IDAHO
SOUTH DAKOTA
WISCONSIN
WYOMING
NEVADA
UTAH
COLORADO
NEBRASKA
IOWA
MICHIGAN
VERMONT
MAINE
NEW HAMPSHIRE
MASSACHUSETTS
RHODE ISLAND
CONNECTICUT
NEW YORK
PENNSYLVANIA
NEW JERSEY
DELAWARE
MARYLAND
CALIFORNIA
ILLINOIS
INDIANA
OHIO
WEST VIRGINIA
VIRGINIA
KANSAS
MISSOURI
KENTUCKY
ARIZONA
NEW MEXICO
OKLAHOMA
ARKANSAS
TENNESSEE
NORTH CAROLINA
SOUTH CAROLINA
TEXAS
MISSISSIPPI
ALABAMA
GEORGIA
LOUISIANA
FLORIDA
ALASKA
HAWAII

Vietnam Veterans Memorial
Washington, D.C.

Vietnam is a country in Asia. In 1954 North and South Vietnam were at war. American soldiers helped South Vietnam fight.

Many Americans did not agree with the war. They did not think American soldiers should fight in Vietnam. The war caused a lot of anger in the United States. In 1973 the United States stopped fighting in Vietnam. The soldiers came home.

Helicopters were used by U.S. soldiers in Vietnam.

Jan Scruggs fought in Vietnam. He was hurt while fighting. After he came home, he thought about friends who had died in the war.

It was hard for soldiers after they came home from Vietnam. They were sometimes treated poorly. Many veterans felt like they didn't fit in. Scruggs thought about how to help.

FACT

Nearly 3 million Americans served in the Vietnam War. Some 58,000 of them died. Many more were injured.

Flags covered the coffins of U.S. soldiers killed in Vietnam.

Planning a Memorial

Scruggs wanted to **honor** the veterans. In May 1979, he started a committee. This group raised money for a memorial. The memorial would honor those who fought in Vietnam. The group raised $8 million. Scruggs gave $2,800 of his own money.

honor—to give praise or show respect

Jan Scruggs in 1982

A contest was held to send in a design for the memorial. More than 1,400 drawings arrived. A drawing by 21-year-old Maya Ying Lin was chosen. She wanted a wall shaped like a "V." The names of the people who died would be carved into the wall.

A drawing of Maya Ying Lin's plan for the Vietnam Veterans Memorial

Jan Scruggs, Maya Ying Lin, and project director Bob Doubek hold a model of the final plans for the memorial.

On March 26, 1982, a ceremony was held to begin work on the memorial. Veterans helped dig where the memorial would stand.

Granite blocks were shipped from the country of India to the U.S. state of Vermont. Workers polished and cut the blocks into **panels**. Names of soldiers who died or were missing were carved into the panels.

panel—a flat piece of material made to form part of a surface

Vietnam veterans used shovels to break ground at the memorial site on March 26, 1982.

About the Memorial

The memorial opened on November 13, 1982. Veterans marched down Constitution Avenue in Washington, D.C. More than 150,000 people went to the opening. They looked for names on the Wall. It was an **emotional** celebration. People would always remember those who had fought in the war.

FACT
A Wall was made for people who cannot travel to Washington, D.C. It is a little more than half the size of the memorial. This Wall travels all over the United States.

emotional—having or causing strong feelings

In 1984 *The Three Servicemen* statue was added to the memorial. It is a statue of three men. The men look like they are walking out of the jungle. The statue shows that many races fought in the war.

In 1984 the Vietnam Women's Memorial Project began. It honors the 10,000 women who went to Vietnam as nurses and in other jobs. The names of eight women who died appear on the Wall. A statue was added in 1993.

Vietnam Women's Memorial

The Three Servicemen

Visiting the Memorial

The Vietnam Veterans Memorial is open 24 hours a day. People sometimes make rubbings of names. They use paper and pencil to trace over them.

The Vietnam Veterans Memorial fulfilled Scruggs' dream. People have a place to remember those who served and died in the Vietnam War. It is one of the most visited memorials in Washington, D.C.

About the Vietnam Veterans Memorial

The Wall
Material: Black granite
Length: 493 feet, 4 inches (150.4 meters)
Height: 10 feet, 1.5 inches (3.1 m) at its highest point.
Cost: $4,284,000

The Three Servicemen Statue
Material: Bronze
Height: 7 feet (2.1 m)
Cost: $4 million

Vietnam Women's Memorial
Material: Bronze
Height: 8 feet (2.4 m)
Cost: $4 million

Glossary

emotional (i-MOH-shuh-nuhl)—having or causing strong feelings

honor (ON-ur)—to give praise or show respect

memorial (muh-MOR-ee-uhl)—something that is built or done to help people remember a person or event

panel (pan-UHL)—a flat piece of material made to form part of a surface

serve (SURV)—to work as a member of the armed forces

veteran (vet-ur-uhn)—a person who served in the armed forces

Read More

Phi, Bao. *A Different Pond.* North Mankato, Minn.: Capstone Young Readers, 2017.

Snyder, Robert C. *What Is a Veteran, Anyway?* West Bay Shore, N.Y.: Blue Marlin Publications, Ltd., 2016.

Internet Sites

Use FactHound to find Internet sites related to this book.

Visit *www.facthound.com*

Just type in 9781543531329 and go.

Check out projects, games and lots more at
www.capstonekids.com

Critical Thinking Questions

1. Why did Jan Scruggs want a memorial for Vietnam veterans?

2. Why were the other two statues added to the memorial?

3. Can you think of other ways the U.S. people honor veterans?

Index